Fred the Firefighter

Felicity Brooks

Illustrated by Jo Litchfield

Designed by Nickey Butler

Fire Brigade Technical Advisor:
Andy Pickard

This is Fred the Firefighter.
His job is to put out fires and
help people in an emergency.

Fred works at a fire station
with a crew of other firefighters.
Pete is their captain.

Judy

Mike

Steve

Anna

Pete

When he arrives, Fred puts on his uniform.

Thick jacket

These strips glow in the dark, so Fred can always be seen.

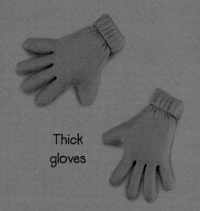

Thick gloves

This visor protects Fred's face in a fire.

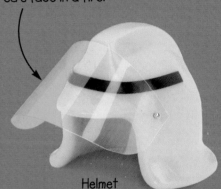

Pants with suspenders

Heavy boots

Helmet

Fred's crew stands in a line.

Pete makes sure they are all there and inspects their uniforms.

3

This tower is at the back of the fire station.

Now it's time for a drill. This is when the firefighters practice all the things they might need to do in an emergency.

Today they practice a rescue with a ladder.

Fred is helping to lower a dummy down the ladder on a stretcher.

Mike and Anna are keeping the ladder steady.

They check all the equipment
and tools on the fire engine.

These long ladders
help the firefighters
reach high places.

Judy is checking the
pump at the back
of the engine.

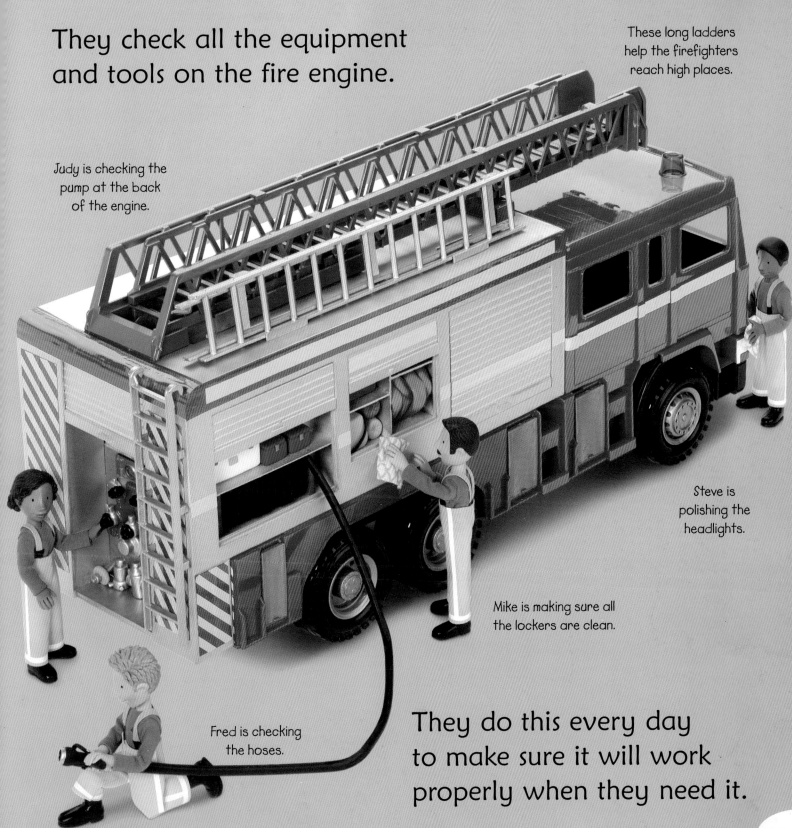

Steve is
polishing the
headlights.

Mike is making sure all
the lockers are clean.

Fred is checking
the hoses.

They do this every day
to make sure it will work
properly when they need it.

At last it's time for the firefighters to have lunch. "I'm starving!" says Judy.

She unwraps a sandwich and is about to take a bite when...

RING!!!

They rush to get ready.

Pete tears a message off the printer.
"House on fire on Randolph Avenue,"
he calls. "There may be people inside."

Mike and Judy heave open the big station doors while the others jump on the engine.

FIRE STATION

Then as soon as they are all aboard, they are off! Pete turns on the siren and the flashing lights.

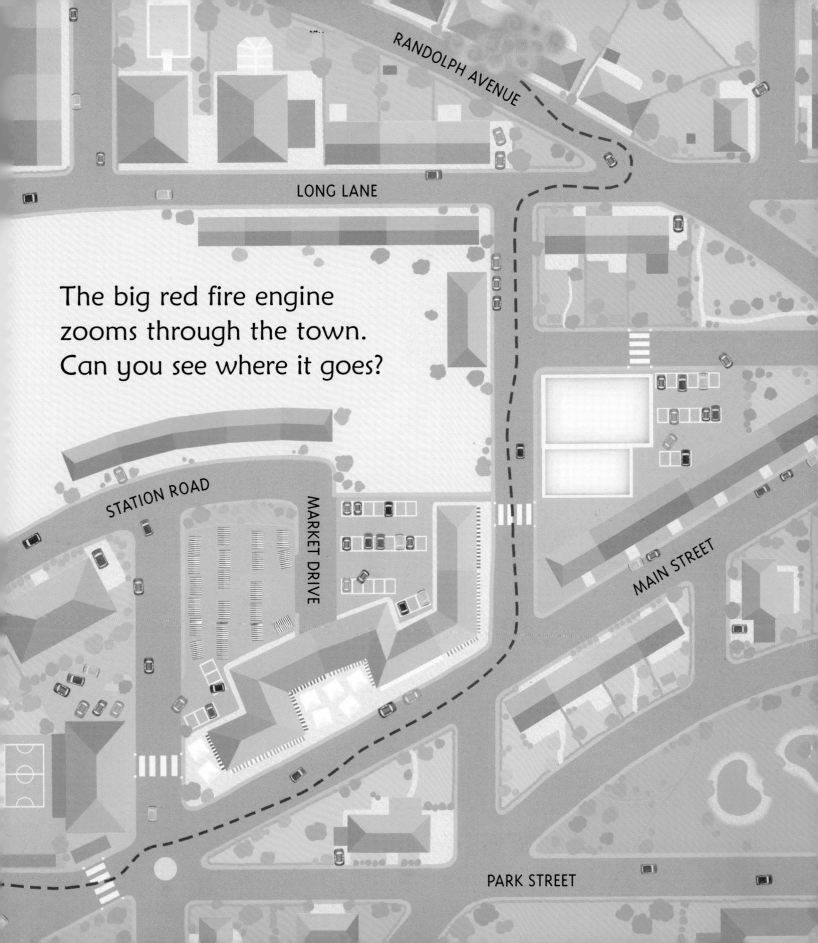

The big red fire engine zooms through the town. Can you see where it goes?

RANDOLPH AVENUE

LONG LANE

STATION ROAD

MARKET DRIVE

MAIN STREET

PARK STREET

They can smell smoke as soon as they arrive at the house. A woman and a little girl rush up.

"We got out, but the door slammed shut and our dog Patch is trapped inside," the woman tells Pete, very upset.

They can all hear barking from somewhere inside the house. Pete quickly figures out what to do.

Steve and Anna must go inside to put the fire out. It's very smoky, so they'll need breathing apparatuses. They put their face masks on.

The others will work from the outside to try to rescue Patch, but first Fred has to smash open the front door.

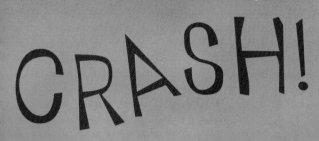

CRASH!

The lock breaks and the door crashes open. Thick, black smoke pours out.

Steve and Anna go in with their hose to attack the fire. It's in the kitchen at the back of the house.

Outside, an ambulance and a police car have arrived. Everyone watches as the firefighters work.

The police use tape to stop people from getting too close to where the firefighters are working.

This board shows how long Steve and Anna have been inside and how much air they have left.

"Look! There's Patch!" shouts the little girl suddenly. "He's in the bedroom."

"Get a ladder," calls Pete.
Fred and Judy carry a ladder
to the house and put it up.

"Please save Patch,"
begs the little girl.
"I'm sure he'll be
fine," says a
police officer.

Judy holds the ladder
while Fred climbs up to
the bedroom window.

He feels excited, but also a little worried.
Lots of people are watching as he reaches the top.

Fred looks through the
window and sees Patch.
"I can reach him," he shouts.

"Keep your visor
down," he calls to Judy.
Then he smashes the
window with his ax.

Fred clears away the broken glass, then leans through the window to rescue Patch.

Just as Fred reaches the
ground, Anna and Steve
come out of the house.
"The fire's out," says Steve,

The little girl
hugs her dog.
"Better get him to
the vet," says Fred.

The firefighters get ready to leave.

Pete goes to find out
what started the fire.

Judy rolls up
the hoses.

Fred puts all the equipment away.

21

"A pan of eggs started it," Pete tells Fred.

"That reminds me," says Fred,
"we still haven't had our lunch!"

Firefighter words

Breathing apparatus – the equipment that firefighters use to breathe fresh air when there is a lot of smoke.

Captain – the person who is in charge of a crew of firefighters at a fire station and during an emergency.

Emergency – something such as a fire or an accident that happens suddenly and can be dangerous.

Equipment – the things that people need to help them do their jobs.

Drill – the time when people practice things they may need to do in an emergency.

Dummy – a piece of equipment shaped like a person that rescue workers use in drills.

Face mask – the part of the breathing apparatus that fits over someone's face.

Pump – the machine at the back of a fire engine that pushes water through hoses to put out a fire.

Siren – the very loud warning noise that fire engines, police cars, ambulances and other rescue vehicles make.

Stretcher – a piece of equipment that rescue workers use to carry people who have been injured.

Fire safety

- Never play with matches, lighters or candles.
- Get an adult to put smoke alarms in your home and test them every week.
- Don't go near a fire or stove.
- Don't leave toys or clothes near a fire, or on top of a heater.
- If you discover a fire, get out, stay out and dial the emergency number.

Photography: MMStudios

With thanks to Oxfordshire Fire and Rescue Service, UK,
and to Staedtler UK for providing the
Fimo® material for models

www.usborne.com
First published in 2004 by Usborne Publishing Ltd.,
Usborne House, 83-85 Saffron Hill, London EC1N 8RT, England. Copyright © 2006, 2004 Usborne Publishing Ltd.
First published in America 2004. AE.